D0660464

FROM THE
RESURRECTION
TO HIS RETURN

FROM THE RESURRECTION TO HIS RETURN:

LIVING FAITHFULLY IN THE LAST DAYS

D.A. CARSON

CHRISTIAN
FOCUS

Copyright © D.A. Carson 2010

paperback ISBN 978-1-84550-577-6
ebook ISBN 978-1-84550-680-3
Mobi ISBN 978-1-78191-044-3

10 9 8 7 6 5 4 3

First published in 2010
Reprinted in 2010, 2011 and 2015
by
Christian Focus Publications,
Geanies House, Fearn,
Ross-shire, IV20 1TW, Scotland

www.christianfocus.com

Cover design by dufi-art.com

Printed by
Nørhaven, Denmark

Contents

2 TIMOTHY 3:1 – 4:8

Terrible times in the last days

3 ¹But mark this: there will be terrible times in the last days. ²People will be lovers of themselves, lovers of money, boastful, proud, abusive, disobedient to their parents, ungrateful, unholy, ³without love, unforgiving, slanderous, without self-control, brutal, not lovers of the good, ⁴treacherous, rash, conceited, lovers of pleasure rather than lovers of God – ⁵having a form of godliness but denying its power. Have nothing to do with such people.

⁶They are the kind who worm their way into homes and gain control over gullible women, who are loaded down with sins and are swayed by all kinds of evil desires, ⁷always learning but never able to come to a knowledge of the truth. ⁸Just as Jannes

and Jambres opposed Moses, so also these teachers oppose the truth. They are men of depraved minds, who, as far as the faith is concerned, are rejected. [9]But they will not get very far because, as in the case of those men, their folly will be clear to everyone.

A final charge to Timothy

[10]You, however, know all about my teaching, my way of life, my purpose, faith, patience, love, endurance, [11]persecutions, sufferings – what kinds of things happened to me in Antioch, Iconium and Lystra, the persecutions I endured. Yet the Lord rescued me from all of them. [12]In fact, everyone who wants to live a godly life in Christ Jesus will be persecuted, [13]while evildoers and impostors will go from bad to worse, deceiving and being deceived. [14]But as for you, continue in what you have learned and have become convinced of, because you know those from whom you learned it, [15]and how from infancy you have known the Holy Scriptures, which are able to make you wise for salvation through faith in Christ Jesus. [16]All Scripture is God-breathed and is useful for teaching, rebuking, correcting and train-

ing in righteousness, [17]so that all God's people may be thoroughly equipped for every good work.

4 [1]In the presence of God and of Christ Jesus, who will judge the living and the dead, and in view of his appearing and his kingdom, I give you this charge: [2]Preach the word; be prepared in season and out of season; correct, rebuke and encourage – with great patience and careful instruction. [3]For the time will come when people will not put up with sound doctrine. Instead, to suit their own desires, they will gather around them a great number of teachers to say what their itching ears want to hear. [4]They will turn their ears away from the truth and turn aside to myths. [5]But you, keep your head in all situations, endure hardship, do the work of an evangelist, discharge all the duties of your ministry.

[6]For I am already being poured out like a drink offering, and the time for my departure is near. [7]I have fought the good fight, I have finished the race, I have kept the faith. [8]Now there is in store for me the crown of righteousness, which the Lord, the righteous Judge, will award to me on

that day – and not only to me, but also to all
who have longed for his appearing.

1.
LIVING
IN
THE
LAST DAYS

Commonly when the Bible speaks about the 'last days', it refers to the entire period between Christ's first coming and his second. Similarly, the expressions 'last hour' and 'last day' usually refer to the entire period. Thus, when the apostle John writes his first letter he says, 'Dear children, this is the last hour; and as you have heard that the antichrist is coming, even now many antichrists have come. This is how we know it is the last hour' (1 John 2:18).

The idea is that the coming of Christ is so world transforming, now that the kingdom has already dawned, that the old world is petering out; it is coming to an end. We are now, already, in the last days.

When the apostle Paul refers to these last days in the passage from 2 Timothy, he is not telling Timothy to write down something that will be only for some future generation. The context shows that Paul is giving instruction that tells Timothy what to do now, in his own time: 'But mark this: there will be terrible times in the last days' (3:1).

More than just 'difficult' times: the word Paul uses, here rendered 'terrible', suggests violence or wild conduct. It's the term that is used, for example, of the Gadarene demoniac. There will be uncontrollable times, wild times, in these last days.

So what will be the characteristics of the ungodly that warrant such a label? In verses 2-5 Paul lists eighteen individual items and then adds a clause to give a nineteenth trait. The first four in the list depict selfishness. People 'will be lovers of themselves, lovers of money, boastful', and 'proud'. According to the Lord Jesus, the first commandment is to love God with heart, soul, mind and strength. The second is to love our neighbours as ourselves. By contrast, these people are characterised first and foremost by loving themselves.

The reason the commandment to love God is first – that is, first in importance – is because it's the one that we always break when we break any other. Whatever we do that is wicked demonstrates that we do not truly love God. The antithesis of loving God is worse than not loving God: it is loving something else supremely, most commonly ourselves or things that we covet. We become idolators: we do not love God supremely. Wallowing in self-love, it is easy to be boastful and arrogant.

The next two terms suggest socially destructive behaviour. We become 'abusive', whether in word or deed; 'disobedience to parents' characterises our conduct. Such behaviour to parents is not the only dis-obedience we manifest, of course, but it reflects a certain kind of rebellion of heart that is fundamentally against God himself. It is true, of course, that authority, even parental authority, can be abused and abusive, but then it is no response to be suspicious of all authority, for some authority is ordained by God. Disobedience to parents becomes a kind of benchmark: where there is disobedience to parents there is almost always a disobedience to all structure, a sort of in-your-face anarchy that is no less an anarchy against God.

Then, in Paul's listing, there are four 'un' words, that is, words that mark literally the absence of something: ungrateful, unholy, unloving, unforgiving. This list shows that sometimes sins manifest themselves in the absence of good, of virtue. What is missing is gratitude, holiness, love, and forgiveness.

Two more characteristics of the age follow these 'un' words. These are sins that reflect speech and behaviour: people become 'slanderous' and 'without self-control'. Self-control is a virtue that is constantly stressed in Paul's three pastoral letters (1 and 2 Timothy, and Titus). In 2 Timothy 1:7 we are told that God has not given us a spirit of fear but of love, of power and of self-control.

Paul then lists two more 'un' terms. It is difficult to translate them into English in this form because our language doesn't always use words the same way that Greek does. 'Brutal', some translations have it: that is, untamed, savage. 'Untamed' is a word that can be used to describe fierce lions and people who act like them. 'Not lovers of the good', our translations say; that is, unloving of the good. These people may love all kinds of things: they may love their own glory, their own self-promotion; they may love their money, their home, their children. But they do not love the good. They do not cherish and cleave to what is truly good, just because it is good.

There follow four items that show perhaps that Paul is moving from characteristics of the age to the false teachers themselves whom he is confronting in his letter. He calls them 'treacherous', 'rash' (or impetuous), 'conceited' and 'lovers of pleasure rather than lovers of God'.

This 'treacherous' category is important. The church is usually not too badly troubled by teachers who are, from the beginning, outside the framework of confessional Christianity, teachers who are saying all kinds of things that Christians view as foolish, dangerous, or simply false – because they're recognised as moving in another circle, they're bringing another set of assumptions. By contrast, if you find someone who has been a public teacher of Christianity for some time and who then gradually moves away from the centre of the faith, it sometimes takes a while to discern the nature of the drift. When the first people to notice begin to wave a red flag, others say, 'Oh, come on, you're being much too critical. After all, we trust this person; he's been such a huge help to us.' It might take a very long time before many people clearly see how serious this drift is.

Such teachers, then, are traitors. They have turned their backs on what they once taught and defended, and so they have become treacherous. It is not uncommon for such people to become rash. They become impetuous in the sense that they do not think through the long-term effects of the stances that they are now adopting. They become conceited, far too impressed by their own new-found opinions and deeply persuaded that the people whom they have left behind are narrow-minded and bigoted. With egos the size of small planets, they become unwilling to think through things out of a confessional heritage anymore; they are too busy telling everybody else how wrong they are. But where is God in such behaviour? It is tragic to find unambiguous examples of people who are 'lovers of pleasure rather than lovers of God'.

Paul's list ends with a clause rather than with a single word or two. The people who make up this lost and condemned age during these last days have 'a form of godliness': they may sport a certain appearance of godliness but they deny its power. This appearance of godliness can have many different shapes. It may be fine liturgy or it may be a lot of exuberant noise. It may bubble over in a lot of fluent God-talk. What is missing, however, is the transforming power of the gospel that actually changes the lives of people. To deny the gospel's power is not necessarily an overt verbal denial of such power. The focus, in this context, is not on verbal denial so much as on the absence of any evidence of power in one's life. Thus in Titus 1:16 certain people 'claim to know God, but by their actions they deny him'. In other words their religion is rich in form and verbal profession, but what is missing is the transformed life. This is tragic.

'Have nothing to do with such people,' Paul now says (3:5). Clearly if you were to apply that maxim to anyone who ever displayed any of these sins you would have to excommunicate everyone, beginning with yourself. The result would not be a small church; there would be no church. Yet Paul's point is surely important. It is built on the assumption that when the gospel comes to us it actually does change people. The gospel does not simply declare us to be just on the ground of what Christ has done, for salvation is more than justification. Salvation includes regeneration, Spirit-empowered transformation of life, such that Jesus himself can say, 'By their fruit you will recognise them' (Matt. 7:20). This does not mean that Christians achieve perfection in this life. It does mean, however, that where there is a pattern of ongoing, unreduced, public sins, a pattern that everybody can see is antithetical to the gospel, at some point you have to say, 'Why should we think these people are Christians if they live in a way indistinguishable from the world? That's not Christianity!' Or, as Paul here puts it, 'Have nothing to do with such people.' This does not mean we should not make friends with them, nor that we should not evangelise them, still less that we should not be civil with them. It means that the church, the body of Christ, must not be made up of such people.

In the final paragraph describing these false teachers, Paul talks about the predatory nature of some of them. They are the kind who 'worm their way into homes and gain control over gullible women, who are loaded down with sins and are swayed by all kinds of evil desires, always learning but never able to acknowledge the truth' (3:6-7). Do not misunderstand this passage. It is no more saying that all women are gullible or weak-willed than it is saying that all men are predators. On the other hand it is certainly saying that you can have a confluence of evils that is morally catastrophic.

I have been involved with more than my share of ministers who have been dismissed from the ministry because of adultery. In almost no case has it been a simple matter of lust. Doubtless there has been a fair bit of that too, but usually the defection is more complex. The minister wants to feel needed; he wants to exercise a certain kind of power. On the other side there may be a desire to be attached to a powerful figure, to feel strong and cherished because of being identified with someone who is at the front. This mutually-reinforcing combination of sins and neuroses, connected with sexual desire on both sides, is a recipe for moral catastrophe. In other words, you may be a false teacher not only by saying things that are not true, but also by hungering for power and conquest that frankly leads to predation. They are the heirs of countless generations of earlier false teachers, such as Jannes and Jambres (3:8), names traditionally assoc-iated with experts who opposed Moses in Exodus 7:11-12. They are teachers who really cannot see and live the truth because they have 'depraved minds' (3:8).

Mercifully, 'they will not get very far because, as in the case of those men, their folly will be clear to everyone' (3:9). Sooner or later the truth comes out; sooner or later the falseness and corruption become clear. This exposure is not always instantaneous; indeed, it may not always be rapid. But sooner or later the truth will out and people will begin to discern what is going on.

Not too surprisingly, some people have accused Paul of being unrealistically negative in this passage. Doesn't the world contain a lot of good? Isn't the apostle himself able to talk about what theologians refer to as common grace, grace commonly given to people everywhere? Yet if one remembers how the apostle is weighing matters, not by sociological standards but by the massive distance from what would be the case if God and his truth were at the centre of everything, one must conclude that Paul is probingly accurate in his criticism. He is not going after the civilised face that we put on, but after the heart of human beings who are apart from the gospel of Jesus Christ. The longer you live, and the more you probe into people's lives, the more you discover that this is a painfully accurate picture.

Now what do you do about it?

2.
HOLD
THE
RIGHT MENTORS
IN
HIGH REGARD

Paul turns to Timothy: 'You, however, know all about my teaching, my way of life, my purpose, faith, patience, love, endurance, persecution, sufferings – what kind of things happened to me in Antioch, Iconium and Lystra, the persecutions I endured. Yet the Lord rescued me from all of

them' (3:10-11). The crucial word that shows
the flow of thought is the initial 'however':
'You, however, know all about my teaching
. . .' By contrast with the false teachers the
apostle has dismissed, you, Timothy, are in
a different camp. They are characterised by
this fading world; you, however, must follow
a different course. Instead of being attracted
to the way they go about things, you know
me. Follow me.

Do you ever say to a young Christian,
'Do you want to know what Christianity is
like? Watch me!' If you never do, you are un-
biblical. After all, the apostle Paul can write
elsewhere, 'Follow my example, as I follow
the example of Christ' (1 Cor. 11:1). Many
things are learned as much by example as by
word. Paul understood the point. He therefore grasped that his responsibility was not
only to teach the truth but to live it, precisely
for the sake of stamping a new generation,
here represented by Timothy. Do we not
recognize the principle when we encourage
parents so to live that they model godly vir-

tues to their children? It's not just what the parents say, it's what they do.

'Watch me,' the apostle says, in effect, to Timothy. Timothy, choose your mentor. You 'know all about my teaching, my way of life, my purpose, faith, patience, love,' he continues. It follows that if you are looking around for a good senior mentor you must always ask some fundamental questions. Do not simply say to yourself, 'Oh, that person seems to be making a real go of it. He is a wonderful success, and I just love his personality. I want to be like that.' No, ask something more fundamental. 'You know all about my teaching,' Paul writes. You must therefore ask, 'Does this person I am thinking of follow apostolic teaching? How about his way of life, purpose, faith, patience, love, endurance, sufferings? What are the virtues and experiences in a potential mentor that are worth imitating? Do you see the point? Choose your mentors and then hold those right mentors in high regard. The reality is that, consciously or unconsciously, all of us follow people whether we intend to or not. After all, that is why advertising works! But we shall be wise if we carefully choose our mentors, in line with the priorities of Scripture.

As a chemistry undergraduate at McGill University, with another chap I started a Bible study for unbelievers. That fellow was godly but very quiet and a bit withdrawn. I had the mouth, I fear, so by default it fell on me to lead the study. The two of us did not want to be outnumbered, so initially we invited only three people, hoping that not more than two would come. Unfortunately, the first night all three showed up, so we were outnumbered from the beginning. By week five we had sixteen people attending, and still only the initial two of us were Christians. I soon found myself out of my depth in trying to work through John's Gospel with this nest of students. On many occasions the participants asked questions I had no idea how to answer.

But in the grace of God there was a graduate student on campus called Dave Ward.

He had been converted quite spectacularly as a young man. He was, I suppose, what you might call a rough jewel. He was slapdash, in your face, with no tact and little polish, but he was aggressively evangelistic, powerful in his apologetics, and winningly bold. He allowed people like me to bring people to him every once in a while so that he could answer their questions. Get them there and Dave would sort them out!

So it was that one night I brought two from my Bible study down to Dave. He bulldozed his way around the room, as he always did. He gave us instant coffee then, turning to the first student, asked, 'Why have you come?' The student replied, 'Well, you know, I think that university is a great time for finding out about different points of view, including different religions. So I've been reading some material on Buddhism, I've got a Hindu friend I want to question, and I should also study some Islam. When this Bible study started I thought I'd get to know a little more about Christianity –

that's why I've come.' Dave looked at him for a few moments and then said, 'Sorry, but I don't have time for you.' 'I beg your pardon?' said the student. 'Look,' Dave replied, 'I'll loan you some books on world religions; I can show you how I understand Christianity to fit into all this, and why I think biblical Christianity is true – but you're just playing around. You're a dilettante. You don't really care about these things; you're just goofing off. I'm a graduate student myself, and I don't have time – I do not have the hours at my disposal to engage in endless discussions with people who are just playing around.'

He turned to the second student: 'Why did you come?'

'I come from a home that you people call liberal,' he said. 'We go to the United Church and we don't believe in things like the literal resurrection of Jesus – I mean, give me a break. The deity of Christ, that's a bit much. But my home is a good home. My parents love my sister and me, we are a really close family, we worship God, we do good in the community. What do you think you've got that we don't have?'

For what seemed like two or three minutes, Dave looked at him. Then he said, 'Watch me.'

As it happened, this student's name was also Dave. This Dave said, 'I beg your pardon?' Dave Ward repeated what he had just said, and then expanded: 'Watch me. I've got an extra bed; move in with me, be my guest – I'll pay for the food. You go to your classes, do whatever you have to do, but watch me. You watch me when I get up, when I interact with people, what I say, what moves me, what I live for, what I want in life. You watch me for the rest of the semester, and then you tell me at the end of it whether or not there's a difference.'

Dave Two did not literally take Dave Ward up on his offer: he didn't move in with him. But he did keep going to see him. Before the end of that semester he became a Christian, and subsequently a medical missionary overseas.

'Watch me!'

You who are older should be looking out for younger people and saying in effect, 'Watch me.' Come – I'll show you how to have family devotions. Come – I'll show you how to do Bible study. Come on – let me take you through some of the fundamentals of the faith. Come – I'll show you how to pray. Let me show you how to be a Christian husband and father, or wife and mother. At a certain point in life, that older mentor should be saying other things, such as: Let me show you how to die. Watch me.

Those of you who are younger ought to be seeking out mentors who have Paul's characteristics. They know the apostle's teaching; they display mature Christian fruit and conduct. Maybe they have been tested by suffering. They demonstrate love and endurance, patience and faith, joy and steadfastness, a hunger for holiness. In this broken world and sinful world, where in these last days so many siren voices are taking us in different directions, hold the right mentors in high regard.

3.
HOLD FEW ILLUSIONS ABOUT THE WORLD

'In fact, everyone who wants to live a godly life in Christ Jesus will be persecuted,' Paul continues, 'while evil men and imposters will go from bad to worse, deceiving and being deceived' (3:12-13). Paul does not mean that every generation is necessarily worse than every previous generation. He means rather that in every generation, evil people get worse and worse. Pol Pot does not start by butchering one third of the population of Cambodia; Hitler does not begin by gassing six million Jews; Mao Tse-tung does not start off killing fifty million Chinese. The French Revolution starts off with people who are trying to get rid of corrupt authority, and ends up with Robespierre and his Reign of Terror. Evil people get worse and worse.

Do not be surprised, therefore. What is astonishing is that after the bloody century we have just come through, so many people think that if we simply sit around a table and talk we will sort it all out. This attitude is astonishingly naïve. Christians should never, ever, be surprised by evil. While we should always be horrified by evil, we should never be surprised by it. Do not adopt a Pollyannaish view of things. Do not be surprised by evil. Hold few illusions about the world. There are many times we should be horrified – surprised, never.

Our culture does not prepare us for such clear-sighted realism. New views of 'tolerance' multiply so strongly that we begin to think that if we avoid criticising anyone and are really nice to everyone, evil so gross that it shocks and horrifies will be rare. This ostensible niceness is so virulent that even honesty is sometimes sacrificed.

A friend of mine is a Reformed Baptist pastor in the American South. An Orthodox Rabbi moved into his area and he decided he would get to know him. So my friend went to him and asked for some private tutoring in Hebrew, not only to improve his Hebrew but also to make a friend. Eventually they began teaching part-time courses together at the local junior college. One night, as they were driving back home from one of these courses, the Rabbi said, 'You do know, don't you, that you and I cannot both be right in our understanding of what you call the Old Testament?' 'Yes,' my friend replied, 'I know, and I love you.' The Rabbi said, 'All my other Christian friends are trying to convince me that we're all saying the same thing; you're the only one I can trust, because you acknowledge that we're different.'

This world is constantly trying to convince itself that we are all pretty good, that we are all saying the same things, that evil is not an endemic and systemic part of us, and that if we are nice, everything will be all right. Certainly there is no merit in being un-nice! But to hide the disagreements, idolatries, greeds, injustice, God-defying arrogance, materialist hedonism, unbelief, and just plain malice of the world is worse than naïve – it is blind. Christians will look at the rawness of history and the prevalence of evil people who become worse and worse, and they will hold few illusions. This is an essential element of faithful living in the last days.

4.
HOLD
ON
TO
THE BIBLE

'But as for you,' Timothy is told, 'continue in what you have learned and have become convinced of because you know those from whom you learned it ...' (3:14). He received his first lessons in the Bible from his mother and his grandmother, Eunice and Lois, mentioned a little earlier in the book (1:5). You are aware, Paul tells Timothy, 'how from infancy you have known the Holy Scriptures, which are able to make you wise for salvation through faith in Christ Jesus' (3:15). Of course, there is a way of learning the Bible that masters more and more data, that might even memorise a lot of text, but that somehow doesn't see the Bible as a coherent whole that brings us to faith in Jesus. But that was not Timothy's experience. He learned the Scriptures in such a way that he discovered how they are able to make a person 'wise for salvation through faith in Christ Jesus'.

Some who go by the name of 'Evangelical' view the Bible in such scrappy atomistic bits that they can find moralising lessons here and there, but cannot see how the Bible gives us the gospel of Jesus Christ. But the Bible is not a magic book, as in: 'A verse a day keeps the devil away'. It is a book that points us to Jesus, and this Jesus saves and transforms. This Jesus by his death and resurrection con-stitutes the good news that men and women may be reconciled to the living God. Here in this book there is instruction on what God has done in Christ Jesus; here there is the message of Christ dying for sinners, of whom I am chief; here there is the promise of the Holy Spirit given in down payment of the ultimate inheritance; here there is transformation. These Scriptures make you 'wise for salvation'.

Indeed, Paul goes on to say, 'All Scripture is God-breathed.' Paul is not saying that the writers of Scripture are inspired by God, though doubtless in some sense that is true; rather, he is saying that the text itself is, finally, God-breathed. God has many different ways of inspiring texts, various ways in which he has given his Word to the writers of the Old Testament and the New. The result is however in every case the same. This Scripture, this written material, is itself God-breathed. In consequence it is 'useful for teaching, rebuking, correcting and training in righteousness, so that all God's people may be thoroughly equipped for every good work.'

In a world where there are many false ideas – many deceptive, selfish and anti-God ideas – what must we do to get orientated toward God himself? We go to God's Word – we hold on to the Bible. We desperately need to think God's thoughts after him. Isn't this what Paul assumes elsewhere? He writes to the church in Rome and tells them not to be conformed to the world, but to be transformed by the renewing of their minds (see Romans 12:1-2). And that means we must hold on to the Bible, not as a magic book, but one that teaches us how to think and what to think, one that provides an entire frame of reference. It is not that this frame of reference saves – only Jesus saves, not ideas about him. But if we understand what this gospel is, and look at all of the world around us out of the framework of this gospel and this book, then we are able to withstand the subtle allure of passing fancies that drive us away from the God who is our Maker, Redeemer and Judge. Hold on to the Bible.

5.

HOLD
OUT
THE BIBLE
TO
OTHERS

Paul's outpouring to Timothy takes us into chapter 4 of his letter. The opening lines find the apostle making an astonishingly powerful plea to teach the Bible to others. 'In the presence of God and of Christ Jesus, who will judge the living and the dead, and in view of his appearing and his kingdom, I give you this charge …' (4:1). It is difficult to conceive of a more spectacularly emotional plea than this, as a way of introducing the charge Paul is about to lay on Timothy. And the charge itself is: 'Preach the word; be prepared in season and out of season; correct, rebuke and encourage – with great patience and careful instruction' (4:2).

Now I know that this is given to an individual – Timothy – and then, in principle, to other pastors. Yet there is a sense in which this is also given to all Christians. Does not the Great Commission itself tell us that we are to make disciples of all the nations, baptising them in the name of the Father, the Son, and the Holy Spirit, and teaching them what Jesus has commanded (see Matt. 28:18-20)? This is teaching ministry, whether it is in our home, in small groups, with our children, or when it is one-to-one. Across the back fence, around the coffee urn at work, in evangelistic Bible studies, or during adult Bible classes, Christians constantly are to be teaching and declaring the Word of God.

In some measure, everything that has been said before this point is essentially defensive. We follow the right mentors so that we will not go astray; we hold few illusions about the world that has so many corruptions in it; we hold onto the Bible so that our thinking does no go astray. But now for the first time we have something that is essentially and strategically offensive – we hold out the Word to others. How else shall we respond to this world that is going off in other directions? How else shall we prevail in the last days?

We hold out the Word to others. We therefore think aggressively in terms of teaching the Word of God in every domain of our lives, and through every channel of the church, until men and women come under the sound of the gospel and very many are converted. Indeed, in this regard, Paul sees himself as part of a long chain. Have you noticed how this section ends in verses 6-8? 'For I am already being poured out like a drink offering, and the time for my departure is near.' This is the last letter that has come down to us from Paul's pen; he is about to die a martyr's death under the Roman Emperor Nero. 'I have fought the good fight,' he continues, 'I have finished the race, I have kept the faith. Now there is in store for me the crown of righteousness, which the Lord, the righteous Judge, will award to me on that day – and not only to me, but also to all who have longed for his appearing.' Do you see? He is passing the torch to Timothy. He is going off the scene and he understands that as he will receive this crown of righteousness, so ultimately Timothy will as well, provided he in turn presses the fight with similar faithfulness.

When I was a a young man I spent quite a lot of time reading some of the writings of John Stott, Martyn Lloyd-Jones, Jim Packer and others who were viewed as giants in the land. Now of course that generation has either retired or died. A few are still productive, but not many. Now I am sixty. I am no giant in the land, but in another twenty or thirty years, maybe a good deal less, I will not be here either. Who then is coming along behind me? Who in turn will succeed that person? And on, and on, and on.

In the light of Paul's charge to Timothy, one begins to see one's ministry not only in terms of teaching the Word right now, but as part of passing God's truth along to another generation that comes along behind us and takes up the reins, proclaiming this same gospel to yet another generation, world without end, until Jesus himself comes back. This chain that stretches forward also stretches backwards, all the way to the apostle Paul. This is the chain that Paul has already told Timothy to construct. Two chapters earlier he wrote, 'And the things you have heard me say in the presence of many witnesses entrust to reliable people who will also be qualified to teach others' (2:2). Now you begin to see how your ministry in your homes, how your handling of this Word as you hold it up to others, how your teaching of a Sunday school class, constitutes part of this massive chain that connects us all the way back to the New Testament, and prepares the people of God for the return of Jesus Christ at the end.

That is how Christians live and work in the last days. We hold out the Bible to others.